Poems Plain and Simple

To Liz
with
special Regard

mel

Poems Plain and Simple

Mel Negaard

iUniverse, Inc.
New York Lincoln Shanghai

Poems Plain and Simple

All Rights Reserved © 2004 by Merle A. Negaard

No part of this book may be reproduced or transmitted in any form or by any means, graphic, electronic, or mechanical, including photocopying, recording, taping, or by any information storage retrieval system, without the written permission of the publisher.

iUniverse, Inc.

For information address:
iUniverse, Inc.
2021 Pine Lake Road, Suite 100
Lincoln, NE 68512
www.iuniverse.com

ISBN: 0-595-31174-1

Printed in the United States of America

Contents

Foreword xv

PART I   FRIENDS & FAMILY

Early Family Life (1925 and on) 3
High School Memories 5
World War II 6
Commonality 9
My Gang 10
Union and Reunion 11
Grandma 12
It's a Parlor (Not a Living Room) 13
Spoons in A Glass 14
The Button Jar 15
Vacation Time 16
True Friends 17
Climbing the Ladder (One Step at A Time) 18
Your Way 19

PART II   POLITICS & ECONOMICS

Lest We Forget 23
The Nineteenth Century 24
Our Society 25
U.S.A. 26

Who are You, American or What?	27
To the Dissidents	28
The United States of America	29
Our Government	30
America	31
The Clinton Legacy	32
Our President	33
Precedent not President	34
Presidential Confessions	35
So Tired	37
The White House Connection	38
The Community Forum	39
The Chinese Challenge	40
The Stadiums	41
Plastic Money (Boon or Bust)	42
What is a Non-Profit Organization?	43
Bullies	44
Bluffing	45

PART III PHILOSOPHY, RELIGION & EDUCATION

Education Vs. Society	49
Family Decisions	50
The Fisherman	51
Life's Journey and Beyond	52
Life Cycle	53
This Life and Beyond	54
Here to Eternity	55
Life's Goals	56
Life's Song	57

Perfection	*58*
Religion	*59*
Survival or???	*60*
Time	*61*
In Our Dreams	*62*
What's Up	*63*
Prophets	*64*
Lucky Me!	*65*
Choices	*66*
Little Things, What's What	*67*

PART IV   JUSTICE

It's The Law	*71*
Judgment	*72*
The Juice	*73*
Orange Juice	*75*
Vice and Advice	*76*
The N Word	*77*
Yah, Naw, You Bet	*78*
Held Hostage in Mexico	*79*
Privileges Not Rights	*81*

PART V   LANGUAGE & COMMUNICATIONS

The Buzz Word (Y'Know)	*85*
Communication	*86*
Hum and Whistle	*87*
Inspiration	*88*
Who Am I?	*89*
Problems	*90*

Reading and Writing	91
PS. The Silent World	92
What do you call it?	93

PART VI   NATURE, ANIMALS & FARMING

A Dog's Life	97
Down On The Farm	98
Evolution	99
Farmers' Progress (The Twentieth Century)	100
The Good Old Days	101
The Greatest	103
Hard Times	104
Linda Is No Lady	105
Linda's a Baby	106
Mother Nature	107
Nature or El Niño	108
The Weather Report	109
Wild Flowers Bloom	110
Who's the Boss?	111
Our Raven	112
Pets	113
The Old Man and his Dog	114
For the Birds	115
A Rare Bird	116

PART VII   SEXUALITY, LOVE & ROMANCE

Love and Marriage	119
Moonlight	120
Moonlight Romances	121

Belonging	*122*
Maiden's Lament	*123*
Guts	*124*
Marriage	*125*
The Feminists	*126*
Full Circle	*127*
He'n And She'n	*128*
AIDS Vs Asylums	*129*
Sexuality	*130*
The U.S.A. Armed Forces	*131*
Who Harassed Who	*132*

Part VIII   Games & Cars

Billiards	*135*
Dreamers	*136*
Lotto in Chicago	*137*
The World Series (Padres VS Yankees)	*138*
Spike's Slough	*139*
The Orange Crate	*140*
The Look Alikes	*141*
Wheels	*142*
Ode to the Gull	*143*

Part IX   Celebrations, Troubles & Empathy

Congratulations (It is a Boy/Girl)	*147*
Happy Anniversary	*148*
Home Sweet Home	*149*
Post Graduation	*150*
Recovering	*151*

The Silent World	*152*
Pleasantries	*153*
The "Golden Years"	*154*

PART X   CALENDAR IN POETRY

Our Calendar	*157*
1998 and Beyond	*158*
'99 A New Year	*159*
Hello—Goodbye (What is Time?)	*160*
Y2K (Bah Humbug) 12/99	*161*
The Presidential Month	*162*
February Events	*163*
Love Vs Hate	*164*
March	*165*
The Green and Gold	*166*
Spring—Etc. March 2001	*167*
April	*168*
April (Easter and Showers)	*169*
Spring Has Sprung	*170*
Wild Flowers	*171*
May Days	*172*
May	*173*
You Are Special	*174*
To: Ma, MaMa, Mom, and Mothers	*175*
June	*176*
June—Seeds to Sow	*177*
My kids Call Me Dad	*178*
Being A Father	*179*
July—Celebration	*180*

July—Jubilation *181*
August *182*
September '98 .... *183*
It's September *184*
The Fall Season *185*
October—Indian Summer *186*
October—Early Fall 2000 .... *187*
October—Jack Frost *188*
Thanks—Then and Now *189*
A Pilgrim's Friend *190*
Six Months of Winter *191*
December—Businesses Smile *192*
Gifts and Spirit *193*
The Prince of Peace *194*
Love and Caring (The Spirit of Christmas) *195*

Acknowledgements

I thank my wife, Lori, who transcribed most of these poems. Also, I want to thank Lee Suplinskas for her work in categorizing and organizing this volume. I am indebted to Ted and Lori Bair, and Rena Weed for typing many of the poems into computer files. My brother, John, is also recognized for his work preparing this volume for the publisher.

My mother, Myrtle (Pederson) Negaard, took the cover photograph in about 1925. The author is seated next to Pa on the wagon. The location is on the plains near Mobridge, South Dakota, where Father and Mother homesteaded.

Foreword

The world would not suffer if these poems were not read, but there would be less joy. Seriousness, whimsy, humor, compassion, regret, judgment: right or wrong, accurate or inaccurate; these are the observations, opinions, recollections and beliefs of a man who has fully lived 80 to 90 percent of his life.

His prodigious efforts from 1997 to 2003 yielded hundreds of poems on varied subjects. Some are from current events, such as the O.J. Simpson murder trial and the Bill Clinton impeachment hearings. Many poems reflect Mel's philosophical, spiritual and political musings. Also his repertoire includes his fascination with the natural world, including the violence of storms as well as the tenderness of springtime, that nurtures the most delicate seeds. He shows his love of animals: wild birds and pets he has come to know, which have brought him unspeakable joy and comfort. But I think the measure of the poet is reflected most truly when he writes about people he admires and loves: his family and friends.

Mel's life is amazingly rich, not because of great wealth, which eluded most of us; but because of what he has drawn from his life experiences. He was born into a humble farm family in South Dakota in 1922. He was 7 years old when the stock market crashed. The next few formative years were times when family farms were lost, money was scarce and on top of that, the drought of the early 30's raised real concerns for survival. Ten years later the threat of war was on everyone's minds—especially young men just graduating from high school. There was little work in South Dakota. In 1941 Mel went to California to find work in the aircraft factories with a few other young men. Eventually he was drafted into the US Army and served in the infantry in the Philippines. They were trained and poised to invade Japan when the A-bombs on Nagasaki and Hiroshima ended the war. He was assigned to General Douglas MacArthur's Honor Guard in the occupation of Japan until he was honorably discharged from the Army in 1946 at Fort Lewis, Washington.

He returned to South Dakota to do some farming. He married Ann Opsal in 1950. Later, he moved to Independence, Missouri, where he worked at Bendix and other companies. He was one of the first Negaard family members to join the RLDS church. His first marriage ended in divorce. He married Alice Ellis in Albuquerque, New Mexico and helped to raise her two teenage boys, Terry and Brian. They moved to Torrance, California, where Mel worked as a government inspector on such projects as the Saturn second stage rocket. His second marriage also ended in divorce.

He moved to Texas to work on "Swing-Wing" of the FB111. When that task was done he moved to Seattle and worked at the Boeing plant as an inspector for military aircraft and missile contracts. He married Lori Bair, who had three sons. The eldest, Ted Bair was married and on his own. Jerry was in the Navy Seals in Vietnam and Denny was finishing high school.

Mel retired in 1984 and moved to California in 1986, the land of warmth and sunshine—a paradise deserving much praise, and a source of joy for his retirement years. He has lived in Oceanside, California, at the Lamplighter Mobile Home Park ever since.

His first poem was written in 1997, inspired by the death of a favorite brother-in-law. That poem opened an unknown floodgate of creative energy that expressed love and care for his family and friends. It expanded to include commentary on current events and to pose questions and answers on our political, spiritual, technical, sexual and playful state of being.

His poetry spans the carefree independence of a child going skinny-dipping with his brothers in a river in Minnesota, to an infantryman carrying a Browning Automatic Rifle chasing Yamashita's army in retreat in the Philippines. It covers the honor of guarding one of America's most famous Generals in the victory over Japan to working on a team to put man on the moon. Mel has lived a unique life rich in experience. He has overcome adversity and reflects joy in his poetry.

John Negaard

I

Friends & Family

Early Family Life (1925 and on)

Our father's friends, they called him Ray;
And his wife, Myrtle, at home held sway.

The three oldest boys, now 6, 7 and 8;
"Be home by 9, and don't be late."

We learned a lot from an older cousin,
Our leader and mentor, his name—Ole Nelsen.

To the Medberry Woods we were initiated.
And for many summers it was appreciated.

We said, "Mother, we're going to the water."
She knew then it was to the River

Through the Medberry Woods, forming a small pool
Where we skinny-dipped so as to stay cool.

We left home with nothing to munch
And picked gooseberries to eat for lunch.

Mother always said, "Play around the block,
And you be home before nine o'clock."

With our cousin, Ole Nelsen,
We learned a lot, lesson by lesson:

With tobacco and paper and now we know
How to roll a smoke and draw and blow.

When it's winter in the Northern States
Get out the sled and find ice skates.

Clamp-on skates were the main fare
And having shoe skates was something rare.

The clamp on skates kept coming loose
And we'd fall down but, "what the deuce?"

We'd put them back on and tighten 'em up
And we'd go again 'til we went ker-plop.

Our mother, like others, would take a count
To see if the tally was the right amount

Now if the tally is not right,
The search is on with all our might.

With the sibling found, it clears the air.
Of loving concerns of a family's care.

Mel Negaard

High School Memories

I started high school in the fall of '36,
But the school was in some kind of fix.

In May that year the school building burned down,
And classes were held all over town.

All the churches were used and the Hall of Legionnaires
At the Masonic Hall we had to climb the stairs.

In the opera house, in it's great hall
That is where we played basketball.

This continued for two years or more
Until the school building they could restore.

During this period I hardly studied at all.
I spent too much time in Dady's pool hall.

This was a place where we could smoke
And on occasion tell a shady joke.

In the new school our courses were completed.
I felt I was lucky none had to be repeated.

In June of 1940 I was in a dilemma
As to whether or not I'd get a diploma.

I got my diploma by a slim margin.
I think they didn't want me back again.

World War II

My pre-induction physical was June 6th '44.
Roosevelt told Eisenhower, "Let's go to war!"

They invaded France on that very day,
And wanted us trained without any delay.

On October second I was sworn in.
That was when my military service would begin.

To Camp Walters, Texas, I was sent
For 16 weeks of army encampment.

I learned to march and to line up for chow.
That is important in a war, you know.

We learned about rifles and machine guns too,
Because that is what trainees have to do.

After basic training we went to Fort Ord.
The ships were waiting and we all went aboard.

Thirty days later it was the Philippines.
MacArthur had returned to the familiar refrain:

"I shall return," was the familiar phrase.
And all America gave him praise.

Now it is August, and Yamashita's in retreat;
The Philippine victory is almost complete.

We were on amphibious training to invade Japan,
And we were ready down to the last man.

Mel Negaard

The Hiroshima bomb had already been dropped,
And then on Nagasaki and the war stopped.

After the surrender on September second
The 33rd Division secured the land that did not offend.

I was just a Doughboy and could not roam.
I was just waiting to go back home.

In 1945, as I remember,
It was the month of November:

Our company commanders received a request:
"Choose a guard for General Mac Arthur, and he must be the best!"

From each company they would select two
I was one they said would do.

The regimental office printed up the orders
And I was on my way to the General's headquarters.

When the train arrived at the station in Tokyo,
Mac Arthur was not there and neither was his limo.

They put me on this six by six truck
That's when I questioned my good luck.

It was good duty as the army goes.
We had hospital beds and they laundered our clothes.

"Doug out Doug" took care of his own,
But all I wanted was to go back home.

It was September '46 when I left Tokyo.
Two weeks later I was in San Francisco.

On to Fort Lewis, Washington, the separation center;
Back to civilian life I yearned to reenter.

Now out of the service, at last I am free.
This is the kind of life that is meant for me.

Mel Negaard

Commonality

When born our bodies have legs and feet,
Though not functional, are tender and sweet.

The relatives come and the child greet,
Some of them even kiss his feet.

At age one we learn to walk,
And are starting to learn to talk.

The legs and feet give us mobility,
Whether commoners or nobility.

Our arms and hands give us dexterity,
And with our intellect, give us diversity.

With arms and legs and intelligence from birth,
Let us live peacefully while on this earth.

My Gang

As an individual I am alone
I go to school and then go home.

Then one day, as I went along,
Some guys asked me to what gang I belong.

I told them that I had not joined any group
And that is when they started their scoop.

They took my jacket and my Nike shoes
And wanted me to get my parent's booze.

After this experience it's my realization
That joining a gang is for my protection.

I joined the group that was called the NERDS
They were the largest and signed up in herds.

I safely roamed within my area
But outside of it, it could be hysteria.

Now the confrontations and shootings galore
Are we still barbarians as in centuries before?

Why isn't it that in this civilization,
In all our wisdom we come to the realization

That our scholars and our intellect
Still have this interconnect?

Mel Negaard

Union and Reunion

A child is born; it may be me or you
But that is what parents do.

The same happens with sisters and brothers,
Aunts and uncles and many cousins.

The children mature and go out on their own
Soon after they leave, it's scary to answer the phone.

The years go by and though families are dedicated
We always seem to get separated.

In this reunion, it will remind
That we are all of kin or kind

Grandma

There's something special about being a grandmother.
She is unique unlike any other.

She has concerns about her children
Also her in-laws with their every burden.

Then there are grandchildren needing her tender care
When they have problems she is always there.

Her vast experience gained through many years
Can give sage advice and stifle many tears.

She greets them all in her special way
And sends them cards on their birthday.

It's very unique unlike any other
As each of you know, if you're a grandmother.

Mel Negaard

It's a Parlor
(Not a Living Room)

In the large farmhouses there was always a parlor
The kids caught in there they'd go no farther.

There would always be an immediate evacuation
They said it is a "no—no" as the explanation.

It was also used as a music room
Where you could practice your most favorite tune.

It's the country kitchen where we would gather
To eat, visit and discuss the things that matter.

The parlor was reserved for just special occasions
Like baptisms, marriages or musical recitations.

Spoons in A Glass

In the early days in a rural community
The drinking of coffee was like a fraternity.

In mid morning and mid afternoon
The coffee was served—and none too soon.

There was usually cookies or cake
It was there for you to take.

The cream and sugar were also there
To add to the coffee for those who care.

There were also spoons in an ornate glass
To stir the ingredients and to add a bit of class.

The spoons and glass in the center of the table
And so to everyone were readily available.

These brief interludes were nice to take
Now in modern times are called a coffee break.

Mel Negaard

The Button Jar

In the Developing years of the upper mid-west
Money for clothing was scarce at best.

A garment bought new was well worn
Had been patched and sewn when torn.

Sound material was saved for projects afar
And the buttons were put in the button jar.

In the Christian church at the Ladies' Aid
From the button jars many matches were made.

Now as Grandmas go, and Five and Dimes are here,
Grandma's button jars are not so dear.

Vacation Time

It gets exciting planning a vacation
Of things to do and other's recommendations.

The vacation starts with much anticipation
Late planes and traffic are a realization.

When you finally reach your destination
Then your family can begin their relaxation.

But in reality that is not true
Let's go here and there until the day is through.

Returning back home is a pleasure
The familiar surroundings we most treasure.

Mel Negaard

True Friends

A true friend is someone you trust
With your spouse or life when and if you must.

In my lifetime there were just a few
That I did trust who were not true.

It's a fact, true friends must pass the test of time
And they are the ones who are friends of mine.

An honest error a friendship can mend
And will be a friend right up to the end.

When things unravel and there seems no end,
That is when you need a true friend.

If you have friends that are tried and true
Then all you need is just a few.

To have a true friend, you must be one;
Or when needed most, they will be gone.

Climbing the Ladder
(One Step at A Time)

His name is Terry, a New York cop,
After 15 years, he is near the top.

Being outstanding in his sector,
He has been promoted and is now an Inspector.

With a promotion you have the duty,
To shoulder the added responsibility.

Promotions are made on one's qualifications,
Terry, to you we offer our congratulations.

Mel Negaard

Your Way

Why are the odds always in your favor,
And never in mine for me to savor?

Why do I never win a big prize,
And see favor in your adoring eyes?

Twill never happen at this time or day
Because, as you know, I did it your way.

II

Politics & Economics

Lest We Forget
Upon visiting Fort Rosecrans Military Cemetery

There is a Roadway through Fort Rosecrans
That may not impress you at first glance.

The manicured ground on each side of the ridge
Was almost like you were crossing a bridge.

The headstone markers were there row after row
And to me, I thought each one a hero.

Now, as I reflect on the Rosecrans Scene,
I'm humbled and awed by what they mean.

Many of us forget what our Freedom cost
But each headstone represents a life lost.

The Nineteenth Century

In the early years there were oxen and horses.
There were, as well, some other resources.

The winds were harnessed for the sail and mill.
They would serve man at his will.

The steam engine Fulton brought about.
Many old things were changed a lot.

The wind-powered ships were now using steam.
The doldrums, a sailor's dread, now only a dream.

It was a large steam pot on a track we now call a train,
That accelerated access to our western terrain.

The gasoline engine did not reach it's potential
Until in the next century. It would become essential.

The nineteenth century inventors were to set the stage,
They created the basis for the mechanical age.

Mel Negaard

Our Society

We have the sun and planets in space
And now enters the human race

We now have the technology
And we also have the rocketry

To send probes to the moon and mars
And other planets and maybe the stars

But here on Earth with all its technology
Most of our people live in poverty.

U.S.A.

In this world and our society
There are individuals and there is FAMILY.

Our family was foreign-born and sought freedom and liberty
Guaranteed in the constitution, which we called democracy.

Our forefathers came here to escape repression
From the countries that enforced these conditions.

Though we were a minority and of Scandinavian descent
We never asked the government for a cent.

As US citizens we wanted the chance
By our endeavors we could advance.

It will not be on a silver platter
We need to prepare, that is the matter.

It takes education or skills of the trade
Before you can say, "I've got it made."

Mel Negaard

Who are You, American or What?

I am a Third generation American from Scandinavia.
I do not live there, I live in America.

I give no homage nor pay them a tax,
For living in America I can relax.

The same is true for the Italian,
As well as, those who are Africans.

If in the USA we segregate by nationality,
We will not survive in our unity.

Your visa or passport shows where you were born
Not your ancestors country of origin.

Though our ancestors came from foreign lands,
Being born here, we all are Americans.

So, ethnic groups, think if you can:
If born here you are American.

Tell me your story of where you fit in.
Are you a "what" or an American?

To the Dissidents

It is your choice to live in the USA
There is no law that you have to stay.

Why is it that you are here;
For economic advantage, or was it from fear?

Now those of you from another country
Could go back, just like me.

But I am an American, born in the USA,
And I will live here until my dying day

Now as a citizen, and an American,
Find a better place, and I hope you can.

Mel Negaard

The United States of America

The most advanced country the world has known
Economically, Socially and Militarily; but Politically may be a frown.

"United we stand, divided we fall."
Here is the question, where are we all?

There is divisiveness in our great country.
Will the South rise again as some do decree?

Whenever something is taken from the whole
Part of it is removed and it leaves a hole.

Look at the Soviet Union, a leader in its day;
Now is fragmented and is in decay.

If our dissidents have their sway
Our country also will be in decay.

It has been forecast in prophetic vision
That it will occur by interior division.

Let us be knowledgeable about these power plays
Or we will regret it the rest of our days

The United States, a world power today
But if fragmented, like the USSR, it will decay.

Our Government

In the late thirties when I was high school bound
The main occupation was tilling the ground.

It was post depression and after the drought,
There was a need to feed each mouth.

Our fine government took it in stride
And work and food it did provide.

It was survival for our family and friends
And it was the means that justified the ends.

As it was then, and still is now,
I would pay my way for room and chow.

Now, who am I, as they all go by?
I have paid my way and now say, "bye bye".

Mel Negaard

America

This is our country, a unified nation.
Let us teach Americanism in our education.

Because of the system or that of choice
They would not have a vote or voice.

Our native language, it should abide
And all the others should be set aside.

In speech and print American English is supported.
Other languages should be aborted.

In the future, in United States schools,
The US taxpayer will hold the tools

To curb multilingual education in public schools.
Now, the taxpayer's burden is nothing short of cruel.

Poems Plain and Simple

The Clinton Legacy

There is a bigger problem for the Presidency
Than the situation with Miss Lewinsky.

The Starr reports have more to relate
About the investigation of the travel and filegate.

If these he survives, and is 'home free',
The liars club winner is slick Willie.

Justification to Hillary he's been thinking over
Hoping she believes unlike any other.

His bedroom is seldom used
Because the travel he has abused.

Air Force One is standing by
To honor his whim—no one asks why.

His many flights for fund raisers
Are all paid by the taxpayers.

We'd be better served grounding this guy
And keep Air Force One out of the sky.

America will survive, although a bit shaken,
Because of a man we call Bill Clinton.

Mel Negaard

Our President

We have a President, who is very intelligent,
And most of us know he has a bad bent.

It is about women and his sexuality.
Is it all false or is it reality?

When he dropped his drawers in a room at the hotel,
Paula told him to go to hell.

Taking her advice, and Satan in his mirth,
Advised him to return to earth.

He can make a speech at the drop of a hat,
And can tell us this and can tell us that.

He also is capable of looking you in the eye,
And almost convincing you he is not telling a lie.

He has his Paulas, but I have to agree
He has done a good job governing our country.

Precedent not President

Our President's agenda from the White House tower
Gives the President International power.

He is not perfect, just like you and me
But has a problem when going to pee.

The Presidents activities must be justified
And from the media he cannot hide.

If to the Americans he is not true
He will have to answer to me and you.

He is intelligent—that is a given
How long can lies keep the polls a winnin'?

Liars are always caught in their trap
And all their stories turn to crap.

And so it is with our President
He has not set a precedent.

Mel Negaard

Presidential Confessions

There is a young woman and her name is Monica
She is accused of playing Bill's harmonica.

Bill is known to play the saxophone
But lets others play when away from home.

But Bill got caught in the White House
Playing with Monica, unknown to his spouse.

But on this day Bill has admitted
That to Monica he had submitted.

With this confession to the whole country
How will this effect Chelsea and Hillary.

With Buddy and Sox there is no question
They do not enter into the equation.

Now on to vacation to Martha's vineyard
Because of the confession, Bill took it hard.

Monica Lewinski did not go along
Hillary thought it would be wrong.

The President's plane; Bill's family aboard;
The vacation at vineyard might be torrid.

When they get back Bill may confess
He made the spots on Monica's dress.

Now the story of the cigar episode
And the polish it does erode.

It is the media that stirs the pot
But it is Starr's report for what is or is not.

It is up to Congress to make the decision
If there is to be an executive division.

If it is impeachment or he does resign
Vice President Gore is the next in line.

Our nation's founders provided in the constitution
That our judicial system will demand restitution.

William Jefferson Clinton, now "slick Willie" has broke the law
And he will be going back to Arkansas.

Mel Negaard

So Tired

This has gone so long I am getting tired,
Seems the investigations are getting mired.

These investigations with money at the top,
No one knows where it will stop.

The lawyers will chase a famous name,
It is in order to gain them fame.

The lawyers may not collect all their fee,
But they get exposure on national TV.

We have seen it on many a trial,
And now it is the Clinton denial.

First it was Paula, now Monica and Willie,
It is enough for us to go willie nilly.

As I said before I am so tired,
How long does it take to get him fired?

The White House Connection

We have a man in the White House,
And we wonder if he's a man or mouse.

The rumors are about this and that,
Some think he's a mouse, others say he's a rat.

The investigations are going far,
And are headed by Kenneth Starr.

With thirteen convictions and most are in jail,
There are a few that are out on bail.

We will have to see how this shakes out,
Some people will weep, and others will shout.

Truth will prevail and we know it must,
If there is a penalty it will be just.

The White House man is not named Lincoln,
And so it must be William Jefferson Clinton.

Mel Negaard

The Community Forum

Roger Hedgecock; he does inform
Us about the issues on the community forum.

Not only locally, but on a national scale,
Being informed-reason will prevail.

Being informed is without question
An important part of the equation.

You give your view of a proposition
And hear views of the opposition.

I think, we should appreciate
Being informed as the electorate.

Thanks to you and to KOGO
That you are on AM 600 radio.

The Chinese Challenge
(Remember Pearl Harbor)

The Chinese sounded the gong
And now they own the city of Hong Kong.

Now in Panama are bases one and two
And could control ships passing through.

It is on Taiwan that they have their eyes
And with its resources it would be a grand prize.

Seizing the Suez on their behalf
Would cut our navy in half.

In Chinese philosophy they watch and wait
Lull us to sleep—then it's too late.

Beware the Chinese and their insidious ways
Like—remember the Japanese in the olden days.

Mel Negaard

The Stadiums

The City Council OK'd the contract.
If they did not, they threatened to not come back.

The owners of the Chargers had an ironclad deal
That the city council, they could not repeal.

As I understand it, It is for twenty years
As it is going now twill bring taxpayer's tears.

Unless there is improvement, as far as I can see,
The city of San Diego will face bankruptcy.

It is the business people that will prosper
But they always await the city council's offer.

The city council apparently doesn't count
How much is in the taxpayer's bank account.

Next it is time for the Padres to say
"We need a new stadium in which we can play."

Let's build it downtown the businesses say,
But for its cost we don't want to pay.

It puzzles me when such a city's offer
Puts so much money in the businessman's coffer.

Plastic Money
(Boon or Bust)

In the early days credit cards were a fad,
It was a status symbol the more you had.

Some of us had them, had them galore,
Some of the folders reached to the floor.

It was convenient that is true,
But where is the money when they come due?

The interest rate, it is sky high,
And you are responsible for all that you buy.

On your credit card, the platinum and gold,
You pay the interest on that which is sold.

When will the public come to realize,
That using credit cards, there is no prize.

It is the custom and their policy,
When overextended, try bankruptcy.

Mel Negaard

What is a Non-Profit Organization?

A non-profit organization to us means what?
They are all volunteers and for services don't get squat.

The organizing leaders surely would have us believe
That they are not looters nor do they thieve.

The leaders at the top seek volunteers
To collect monies to cover their careers.

Bullies

There are bullies at many levels
But most are just the little devils.

The little devils do nitty gritty
The big bullies control the big cities.

The biggest bullies with their decrees are meted
With truth and justice evil will be defeated.

As with Hitler and his regime
So it will be with Saddam Hussein.

Mel Negaard

Bluffing

When we were young and tried to bluff
It was not serious, you know, kid stuff.

But now we're older and all grown up.
Now, its money or muscles needed for backup.

Now as a bluffer and going big-time
Your bluff is called and your loss is mine.

So if Saddam is running a bluff,
The US has called, He's to say, "enough is enough!"

Lasting relationships must be honest and true
No room for bluffing, or it's catch 22.

III

Philosophy, Religion & Education

Education Vs. Society

High school graduates, and this is no quirk,
Most are not qualified or ready to work.

The concerned parents send them off to college,
So the sons and daughters can gain more knowledge.

Some 'students' go there to play,
And the parents have them out of the way.

But most are sincere, I have to agree,
They want to excel and get their degree.

Other 'students' go there to play,
Some have to work to pay their way.

Students that work to earn a degree,
It is a tribute to our society.

If the students see the big picture,
It is the ticket to their future.

Family Decisions

As thunder clouds bring the rain,
Our human frailties bring us pain.

When the pain is too severe,
And there is no hope for life so dear,

Your Loved One's decision, that you cannot make,
Is a grievous one they have to take.

It is not with malice. It is with Love.
It is your comfort they are thinking of.

When our lives are over and there is no night
You can tell your loved ones that they did right.

Mel Negaard

The Fisherman

A man named Peter was a fisherman
He made a living and then he met The Man.

And the Man said as calm as could be
"Store your net and boat and follow me."

After the Man said, "Peter, feed my sheep"
Waiting in the garden he fell asleep.

When Pilot declared crucifixion
Peter decided to go fishin'

On that day the fishing was poor
And the Man said, "fish away from shore."

"Follow me, if you can,
I'll make you fishers of man"

Life's Journey and Beyond

When we are born our parents are proud
In spite of our whimpers and our crying out loud.

In our childhood and our early years
We have laughter and we have tears.

The years go by, we go to school and church.
If we do not, we are left in the lurch.

Time goes slowly for most everyone
We can hardly wait 'til we are twenty-one

When that day comes we will have a blast
But in reality it does not last.

We must contemplate: what is our potential?
That which is superfluous and what is essential.

In middle age, if all goes right
At the end of the tunnel we will see a light

In our golden years, may our lives be good
And our many trials can now be understood.

Our days are numbered, as we all know.
When it is our time we will have to go.

Beginnings and endings are in this sphere;
But in eternity, there is no death there.

Mel Negaard

Life Cycle

The little acorn picked up by a squirrel
Was buried down deep in the rich black soil.

The gentle rains and plenty of sun
Caused the acorn to sprout and life had begun.

The seasons passed by and an oak tree did grow.
It weathered the storms and cold winter's snow.

It grows tall, as years come and go,
And the oak's many branches give shade down below.

Now it is mature and drops acorns to be found,
If only a squirrel will plant them in the ground.

This Life and Beyond

In this world there's no guarantee
That you will live to be seventy
Now here I am at age seventy-five
Few people, I know, thought I'd still be alive

My life style, though not the best,
Has bettered the odds of those at rest
If I stay healthy and more years do come
Then they will be more than welcome

If life's fortune is not in my favor
A longer life I do not savor
When I was young I was told
That some day I would be old

It is hard to believe at a young age
That years later you'll be a sage
The years come and go and time goes on
Friends and relatives have passed on

In a few years it will be our turn
To put our ashes in the urn
The spirit lives on and God we pray
We will meet again on resurrection day.

Mel Negaard

Here to Eternity

We have survived for another year
Our life on earth we hold most dear.

It is better, they say, on the other side
But on this earth we long to abide.

We all know for a certainty
We'll not be here for all eternity.

The years go by and things seem fine
But we all know there will come a time

When we must let it go
And be freed of this earthly woe.

Let us be assured, as we surely must,
As the saying goes: "in God we trust".

Life's Goals

Now as a family, I would like to say,
That in the Depression we had feet of clay.

The future was cloudy for one and for all
As each of the mystics gazed into the crystal ball.

Through a humble beginning, our Dear Mother said,
"These kids need a high school Ed."

We were not the smartest but we looked bright
And we paid attention and we turned out right.

Now as seniors we have met our goals
We paid our dues; it heartens our souls.

Mel Negaard

Life's Song

There are first times for all of us
Some are very nice and others we cuss.

Christmas and Birthdays we handle with ease
Valentines and vacations are just a mild breeze.

There are discords as we go along
That breaks the harmony of life's sweet song.

First time occurrences sometimes come in bunches
If so, we must learn to roll with the punches.

To go through this life I've got to admit
It takes fortitude and a lot of grit.

Perfection

You get up in the morning
Just like me
You take a shower
Just like me

You eat breakfast
Just like me
You go to work
Just like me

You go to lunch
Just like me
You go home at day's end
Just like me

You watch the news
Just like me
Later it's to bed
Just like me

How can it be?
You aren't perfect like me?

Mel Negaard

Religion

In this world, life is uncertain
I often wonder what's beyond the curtain
That which we are taught by our religious leaders
If we follow them we will be believers.

In the Christian dogma as they perceive it
And they preach and teach until you believe it
Once I followed a philosophy I thought was true
I gave of my time and my money too.

After many years of religious observations
To the religious leaders we owe our obligations
To them our fortunes and our moneys go
To us their promise of blessings to bestow.

They accept our offerings, Yea, even the widows mite.
But when down and out the purse strings are tight.
The Lord will take care of us as we give our offerings
Even though from the family there may be murmurings.

As with politicians and clergy also
It seems the needs grow and grow
When our spirits leave this sphere
What will our ministers tell Saint Peter?

That what is justified for each entity
They go to heaven or hell for eternity
Can our ministers at the Golden Gate
Influence Saint Peter to say "yea" or "negate"
Our passage to where the cauldrons brew
Or, to where the heavens are blue.

Survival or???

It is interesting to observe and see
The diverse animals on air, land and sea

Some live on the ground others in trees
And there are those who live in the seas

There are animals that traverse all three
But it is only man that has broken free

The engineer's knowledge and the rocket's power
Will put a satellite in orbit in as soon as an hour

We now have nukes that can obliterate
Most living things that on earth habitate.

Mel Negaard

Time

Time is a phenomenon and who does know
Where it comes from and where does it go?

Isn't it strange that tomorrow "today"
Will be known as yesterday?

Tomorrow is coming and as for "yesterday"
We say goodbye, this is a new day.

"I don't have time", is what we say
But have to make it up on another day.

Why is there time on another day
To do the task we could do today?

In Our Dreams

As kids and juveniles, on our parents we depend
For what they can afford for what they can spend.

But as we mature and we leave home,
It is then that we realize the cost to own.

In dreams we fantasize of what life could be;
But in real life we learn it is just a fantasy.

We all have visions of Castles in the Air
Or, of becoming a millionaire.

But the Reality is: there are very few
That attain this goal, other than me and you.

Now we have fine cars and palatial estates,
But, Gee Whiz, we need help to open the gates.

In my waning years I ask what did I miss:
A big stock deal or a loving kiss?

Momentarily, as I depart from life on Earth;
Where is my mark I've made since Birth?

Mel Negaard

What's Up

Scientists tell us what mass is,
But cannot explain what gravity is.

They postulate creation of the universe,
On the big bang theory, let us converse.

Now tell me why the moon and planets are round,
Not obtuse. Can a reason be found?

We know about mass, but what can it be,
And who knows about gravity?

What is the force in our solar system,
That keeps us stable in our galaxy prison?

Prophets

As individuals we may go awry
But as parents we really try

To raise our kids and instill our mores
And if right we will receive the praise.

But there are times, as we all know,
The odds and reason are thrown out the window.

And so it happens with some offspring.
They say it's the genes or that kind of thing.

And so it was with those I knew
They were good people, except for a few.

There was only one that was really bad
And by his action made his kinfolk sad.

A self proclaimed Prophet his followers he led
Purging out the sinners. Now five lay dead.

At his sentencing he did orate
But did not change, death was his fate.

"Beware of false Prophets", we have been told;
And Jeffery Donald Lungren came out of that mold.

Mel Negaard

Lucky Me!

Did my spirit choose of where I would be?
And I chose America?   Oh Lucky Me!

Did I choose my parents that lived in America?
                    Oh Lucky Me!

Now as a senior with a great family living in America
                    Oh Lucky Me!

Now as an octogenarian and still quite healthy
And living in America
                    Oh Lucky Me!

Choices

In every situation we have a voice
For positive or negative we make the choice.

The choices we make throughout the years
Will give us joy or fears and tears.

By our bad choices we have learned;
There's no reward that was earned.

Now as adults with all the lessons learned
Our choices are wiser; the rewards have been earned.

Mel Negaard

Little Things, What's What

I was asked, "You know what?" And I said I did not.
And asked again, "You know what?"
"No, tell me what it's about."
It's the truth, know it or not.
It's little things that it's about.
It may be a wink, and elbow or nudge
That will defuse an argument or a grudge.

We need to know what's hot or not
For it's little things that mean a lot.
But we have to know what's hot or not.
Computers and software: big things they've got.
But in this life little things mean a lot.

IV

Justice

It's The Law

There was a happening that stuck in your craw
And you said, "there should be a law".

That was a saying 70 years ago
Now we have them and even more so.

It's in the home and on the street
And once passed there is no retreat.

We are a Republic; A country of laws
Are we unknowingly becoming the outlaws?

Even the lawyers have to be specialists
To prosecute all laws that are on the list.

Now we have the laws and there are more to come
With each law passed we lose some freedom.

Judgment

Abstract poetry I do not comprehend,
And most people do not understand.

There is no rhyme or meter or tense,
And to most of us it makes no sense.

Poetry to me has rhyme and grace,
And a message in its place.

Rhyme, rhythm or meter is what poems are about,
If this is not true, you can count me out.

The abstract poem that won first prize,
Interpret it for me and make me more wise.

A poem written in ancient lore
We do not understand so it is a bore.

Poetry should not be a mystery,
That we must review ancient history.

Poetry should strike the harmonic strings,
And be the music that harmony brings.

Mel Negaard

The Juice

He was one of the best and we called him O.J.
All of us thought that he was okay.
Football was the name of the game
And that is where he gained his fame.

He could catch passes and down field could run
And quite often score a touchdown.
During his career many would attest
As a running back O.J. was the best.

Now he is retired, the playing days are over
And he should be living in fields of clover;
And so he did for several years
But then came trouble, which brought on tears.

He is a strong man, more than you or I
There was a fight and he blackened her eye.
Nicole divorced him and wrote him a letter
To let O.J. know their lives would be better

To sever wedding vows and our lives remake
For, at least, the children's sake.
As their parents we both must try
To hear their pleas when they cry

Then came that day in nineteen ninety-four
That their mother was no more
Who was it that drew the knife?
That took the children's mother's life?

Poems Plain and Simple

At the criminal trial for this incipient
They did conclude that he was innocent.
O.J. was acquitted in the criminal trial
But in the civil suit he will go the extra mile.

Mel Negaard

Orange Juice

He was an athlete and in college a star,
The scouts predicted that he would go far.
All the pro teams, they wanted him,
And paid him millions to play for them.

He played superbly and made many a score,
And what pro team could ask for more.
When he retired and was in good health,
He had a nice family and shared his wealth.

They seemed happy until that one day,
That this one woman entered the fray
It was then that the wife withdrew,
And told him I am divorcing you.

She got the children and money to support,
All of them in most any port.
The ex husband on a trip to Chicago,
Informed of the tragedy, the golf he'd forego.

He returned to LAX as soon as can be,
Not asking the question, who could it be?
He was a suspect but the jury said no,
Not enough evidence so let him go.

In the civil trial they did portray
Him guilty and made him pay.
The judicial club is very small,
For Fred Goldman there's no money at all.

He was guilty most people say,
He is not innocent and his name is O.J.

Vice and Advice

Using tobacco is bad for you,
Be it the smoking type or the kind you chew.

In public places it's against the law,
To light one up or to take a chaw.

Our politicians say taxing tobacco is best
To provide health coverage for all of the rest.

They give free needles to shoot in the arm,
So their fellow junkies will come to no harm.

Condoms are provided to a large proportion,
Of those sexually active to prevent abortion.

Alcohol is legal and sold in the bar,
And injures more people than tobacco by far.

Is the playing field level, I am asking you,
Did you get to vote on what you cannot do?

Mel Negaard

The N Word

In our society we seem perplexed
About political correctness and what's coming next.

History is fine, but it is passé
That is in the past, this is a new day.

The "N" word now we do not use
If it is uttered is considered abuse.

I don't understand why in all of the regions,
They discriminate against us because we're Norwegians.

Yah, Naw, You Bet

Yah, yah, yah I'm Scandinavian,
I'm here now and am a citizen.

Naw, naw, naw I'm not a Swede,
We fought them and now are freed.

Now here in America we do not fight,
Except at the dance on a Saturday night.

Each girl was pretty, with a fancy hairdo,
To charm her man to say "yah, yah I do".

She got her man, but does not forget,
Whether Swede or Norsk it was yah, yah, you bet.

Mel Negaard

Held Hostage in Mexico

There are places that we can go
Some of us travel to Old Mexico.

Some do not know or are not aware
No guns are allowed, even when declared.

Situations do happen and accidents occur,
But Mexican justice to us is a slur.

Mexico wants tourism but lo and behold,
On any provocation release they withhold.

They hold you hostage 'til money is paid.
This is a fact and is no charade.

The U.S. and Mexico do share a border,
And it's been proven, we are a good neighbor.

For monetary gain Mexico does upstage,
The U.S. citizens, holding them hostage.

The credit cards and U.S. money
Must be exchanged for Mexican currency.

And tourists visiting to Old Mexico
Not knowing the laws, to jail they go.

The Mexican government, they must reform,
That holding hostages is not the norm.

Medical assistance in Mexico is denied
Unless the money you have supplied.

So my advice is take many pesos
Or you may find your tail in jail.

Mel Negaard

Privileges Not Rights

In the United States we have many privileges.
In many other countries they are merely images.

Like owning a plane or even a used car,
It is not realistic to dream that far.

We have to be licensed for a car or a plane
And obey the laws or we suffer the pain.

To lose our license to drive or fly
You then realize a privilege is bye bye.

Obey the laws or else some day
You will be caught and will have to pay.

V

Language & Communications

The Buzz Word (Y'Know)

My socks are worn out, Y'Know; so I went to the store, y'know;
The same place, y'know, I have gone before, y'know.

The sales person came over, y'know. I said I wanted socks, y'know.
The color I wanted were still in the box, y'know.

We got them out, y'know; they were the right shade, y'know.
Then I thought that, y'know, I had it made, y'know.

I took them home, y'know; and to my surprise, y'know.
The socks were, y'know, the wrong size, y'know.

This buzzword could go on, y'know, maybe forever, y'know.
But to curb its use is my endeavor, 'know what I mean?

PS My problem is this, if you already know,
Why do I keep reminding you so?

Communication

In Africa it was the jungle drum
That sent the news of what is to come.

In early America it was the wagon train
That carried the news across the terrain.

Then with progress came the pony express,
It crossed the country in a month or less.

Then came the telegraph with its dot dit dot.
It was very fast and helped a lot.

Then came the telephones and they were fine
If you had a phone plugged into the line.

Then came radio with short wave and CB
And there was talk between you and me.

In no other age have we seen the likes;
TV, E and voice mail via satellite.

What will be next only time will tell
Right now it's changing to the digital.

Next may be brain waves we use to communicate.
If true, a short story I will have to relate.

Mel Negaard

Hum and Whistle

Since the beginning of time man has sought rhythm,
First the hollow logs and then the drum.

Musical instruments evolved from this form,
And now we have winds, bass, strings and horn.

To the 20th century you had to hear it live,
Until the phonograph, which did transcribe.

We used to hum and whistle in our ramblings
Now are those sounds only heard on recordings?

We have Cassettes, CD's, and the radio;
But I ask you, where did hum and whistle go?

Inspiration

I am sitting here awaiting inspiration
It seems my mind is in no condition
To inspire a thought that can be related.
It seems my brain is constipated.
For this reason I cannot
Write down something I forgot.

Mel Negaard

Who Am I?

I am sitting here with pen in hand
And waiting for inspirational command.
Perhaps I'll write something profound,
But the appropriate words cannot be found.

Perhaps then I can coin a phrase
That will give me recognition and praise.

As often is the case, it was not to be;
I will just remain plain old ME.

Problems

There are people who do not delay;
They see a problem and solve it today.

Then there are people who talk it to death;
They talk and talk until they're out of breathe

There are people like me, who procrastinate;
Who put things off—we'll never be great.

Mel Negaard

Reading and Writing

To learn to read opens the door:
The door of knowledge and much, much more.
Writing is a form of the unspoken word,
But as you read it, it is as if you heard.

We use writing for our communication
From person to person as well as nation to nation.

If the written word you do not understand
More qualified people will be in demand.

To record the words that have been spoken
It must be in symbols or letters of token.

If these symbols or letters, say, for instance
We do not comprehend, we are showing our ignorance.

Hey, that is not to say that we are all wrong,
But we should be able to communicate in our native tongue.

Oral and written communication between one another
Are more important than any other.

PS. The Silent World

There is no sound; no call from home,
Because there is no telephone.

There would be no radios or stereo
To watch cowboys go to the rodeo.

At year's end, even with a beer,
We could not shout, "Happy New Year!"

Mel Negaard

What do you call it?

What's this thing, what is its name?
I do not recall much to my shame.

Needless to say, there is many a way
For us to iterate what we wanna say.

So whatever it is we try to convey
You'll understand what we're trying to say.

VI

Nature, Animals & Farming

A Dog's Life

When your master's family is all at home
Everything is peaceful and you remain calm

When strangers approach the house or the farm
You must get up and sound the alarm

When the family leaves for shopping or the show
That is when time really goes slow

You must be vigilant, alert as can be
Because you must guard the property

You may chase your tail or even try to sleep
But it's your duty your guard to keep

But when your family does finally arrive
That is the time you really come alive

You wag your tail and give a bark or two
Which seems to mean welcome home to you

The waiting and watching and all of the dread
Was all worth it when you get a pat on the head

Your master's activities cause canine strife
And that is why it's called "Living a Dog's Life"

Down On The Farm

It was in the summer we moved to the farm,
The wide open spaces held some charm.

There were cattle, horses, hens, hogs and sheep,
And each day, chores that we must keep.

In the summer there was hay to stack,
So through the winter livestock would not lack.

And in the fall it was: harvest the grain,
And also, it was back to school again.

It was a country school, grades one through eight,
And Mrs. Mullroy kept us straight.

There was a path across the field,
That our footsteps the land did yield.

That little path led to the school,
We learned the three R's, that was the tool.

It was the springboard of acceptance not rejection,
For accreditation to higher education.

As a large family and though poor,
We all tried to better the score.

We all realized independent to be,
That education was the key.

That little path to the country school,
And learning the three R's was the tool.

Mel Negaard

Evolution

This is the time of early spring,
And it is the colors that jonquils bring.

It is the time to plant the peas,
It won't be long your palate to please.

Then the string beans that are so tender,
It was a delicacy that I remember.

Earlier it was radishes and then cucumbers,
Now it is tomatoes coming in numbers.

And with all the condiments,
The salads satisfy all the residents.

As humans we survive by land, air and sea,
That humans will survive throughout eternity.

Farmers' Progress
(The Twentieth Century)

In the early 1900's there was a factor,
For the farmers it was horses vs. tractor.

Then McCormicicks and John Deere,
Shifted the age into high gear.

Their tractors and reapers and the combine,
Left horse believers far behind.

Now the mechanical age and all the progress,
It has benefited every one of us.

Just one machine does the work of ten,
But this is now and not back then.

The advances made with automation,
Helps feed the world and also our nation.

Mel Negaard

The Good Old Days

After the roaring twenties came the stock market crash
That is when people lost all of their cash.

The banks closed and if that were not enough,
Most of our country suffered a severe drought.

The only crop the fields would grow
Was Russian thistles which we did mow.

We raked them up and put them in stacks
And hauled them home in our hay racks.

The livestock existed but thistles did not suffice
So our government bought them at its own price.

The government slaughtered them and it seemed just for spite
No one was allowed to take even a bite.

At this time, we were just boys
And much of the time we made our own toys.

In summer we hiked to woods and the lakes
In wintertime we put on ice-skates.

After the drought and we grew older
Heavier chores we had to shoulder.

The planting and harvesting of the corn and grain
To help provide for the family's gain.

The wood supply for winter we'd gather
To keep the family warm that was the matter.

Milking the cows and feeding the chickens
Feeding the horses and the pigs, we were busy as the dickens.

Get the kids off to school, their clothes matching fronts and backs,
Those were made from Mother's best flour sacks.

Hand-rolled smoke or a pinch of Copenhagen
The men all thought they'd died and gone to heaven.

These good old days, the days of yore,
We will never see again, nevermore.

Mel Negaard

The Greatest

This is the greatest state and is so for many reasons,
Among many others, it has four seasons.

In the summer and fall, there is fishing and hunting,
And in the winter there is snowmobiling.

There are great plains and the mountains are high,
And the tallest one touches clouds in the sky.

In this great state there are many resources,
Tourism, fishing and oil, are some of the sources.

In this poem of geography that I'm trying to relate,
How many of you can guess the name the state?

Hint: Our largest state.

Hard Times

In the Depression the rich ate butter
And the poor ate lard,

Wheat bread, made from scratch,
And vegetables from the garden patch.

The laborers worked ten hours a day
With no minimum wage to pay.

The farmers gave them room and board
And whatever they could afford.

During the depression everything was rough.
In order to survive you had to be tough.

Then came the drought, with which to contend.
We prayed for rain, the farmer's friend.

There was no rain and the winds did blow
And brought dust storms from the states below.

The dust clouds were so profound
That a sunray could not be found.

Our tumbleweeds and soil from Kansas
Almost blew down some of our fences.

It was so dry there was no feed
To grow the fodder that animals need.

Mel Negaard

Linda Is No Lady

It's Saturday, and Hurricane Linda is on the go.
It's said she may hit San Diego.

Here we are waiting with bated breath
To learn of her strength and of her width and breadth.

Or if the Rain comes down in torrents.
We'll protect our property as caution warrants.

Linda's a Baby

The morning was overcast and the humidity high;
But Hurricane Linda has not yet passed us by.

Linda is off our coast a hundred miles or so.
We could use some rain as you well know.

Now for today there is no sorrow,
But we don't know what will happen tomorrow.

High tides and storms along this coast
Damage coastal businesses and beaches the most.

With full moon tides and with Linda off shore
Our coastline will be pounded much more.

We did not get the strong winds expected,
Nor the heavy rains that were projected.

Instead we are getting a gentle rain
For which we are grateful to obtain.

Linda's rains are to continue
Until tomorrow, according to the venue.

Linda's bad name, that she's no lady,
Now on the flipside, she's acting like a baby.

Mel Negaard

Mother Nature

Our Mother Nature, sometimes she rages,
As she has always done throughout the ages.

She gives us rain to raise our crop,
Occasionally she forgets and it doesn't stop.

There is flooding and the crops spoil,
There is loss of property, also labor and toil.

She also has wind, snow and ice at her disposal,
That can challenge us and make life miserable.

She has gentle ways like the days in June,
And in the fall is the harvest moon.

As a mother she wants us to stay alive,
And that all creation on Earth will survive.

Poems Plain and Simple

Nature or El Niño

In the summer there was a prediction,
That El Niño would affect our nation.

Changes of climate and of precipitation
Was the consensus of their observation.

Not everyone believed in El Niño,
The storms are here bringing rain and snow.

The strong winds are blowing up a gale
And it accentuates the rain and the hail.

The surf is up and pounds the shore,
The beach sand retreats back to the ocean floor.

It is nature's way, the ebb and flow,
Who is to say he is not El Niño.

Mel Negaard

The Weather Report

We may get 5-10 inches the weatherman stated
If that is true we will be inundated.

Along with the rain strong winds will blow.
They are predicting 50 miles per hour or so.

So now we sit and wait and wait
For Mother Nature to decide our fate.

If we survive and it's not too gory
I will tell you the rest of the story.

Wild Flowers Bloom

For millions of years Mother Nature did provide
A variety of blossoms all over the countryside.

Some years they are scarce, other times plentiful.
You may just get a bouquet or at times a bucketful.

The flower produces seeds that are for regeneration;
That guarantees survival for generation after generation.

Though they have bloomed for eons in the past,
We are the ones who have viewed them the last.

Mel Negaard

Who's the Boss?

I planted it there, just a sunflower seed
When it came forth it was not a weed.
The first two leaves are tender and small
Belying a mature plant that is sturdy and tall.

In about 60 days from top to bottom
This tall sturdy plant is producing a blossom.
It's the blossom center that produces the seeds
That reproduces the species according to nature's needs.

We have photographs that one can show
As this plant matures. And how it did grow!
On average it grew an inch a day
That's growing some, wouldn't you say?

The seed pod and blossom are in they infancy
But when it matures we say, "Oh my, Oh me!"
A sunflower seed pod at 12 inches across
In the plant world, it is the boss.

Our Raven

The ravens nested in the palm tree
Then there were two, now there are three.

When he fledged he stuck out his neck
And came to rest on our front deck.

As a juvenile and as you will see
He always came back to his hatching tree.

Now he has a mate and a nest to be
They strive to build in his favorite tree.

They bring many sticks to make their nest
He is like family—we wish them the best.

Mel Negaard

Pets

To many families who have their pets
And they love them. To others they are pests.

There are canines and real companions
Even though they're not grand champions.

The feline variety at times occur
Jump into your lap and start to purr.

There are talking birds and birds of prey.
The talkers are pets and the others away,

Birds of prey are hunters
For meat and seeds they are scavengers.

Pets brighten days when in solitude
And to them we give our gratitude.

The Old Man and his Dog

Their daily walks were necessarily slow.
The faithful dog knew where to go.

They went forth and soon were back,
They usually travel the same track.

With the walk over the dog gets a treat.
They take a nap, the Old Man is beat.

For the many years they've been together,
The Old Man knows it's not forever.

For now at least they haven't a care
For as companions their lives they share.

Mel Negaard

For the Birds

In this world some animals fly
In migrations some stop by.

Our bird feeders with sugar water we fill.
To attract the Hummers and the Orioles.

Birds are a species that are so free
That they can defy the laws of gravity.

Birds fly around with impunity
And we humans look at them with envy.

Studying bird's flight man has found
That he could also get off the ground.

A Rare Bird

Some things of beauty in hands we hold
And there are others that only can be told.

It is the latter to your attention I draw
To the wondrous beauty of this bird I saw.

The Audubon Society I called on the phone
To report the sighting I had seen at home.

The Hummingbird's body was white as a swan
"It is very rare", said the Audubon.

VII

Sexuality, Love & Romance

Love and Marriage

The lovers married and had big dreams
Of a new home and car within their means.

Like most of us, salaries were mid-range.
Then something happened that made a change:

"I'm pregnant", she said, "and I don't mean maybe."
Nine months later they had a baby.

The new addition was very adorable
And soon they wondered if it was affordable.

On one income it was apparent
They needed more income than from one parent.

Mommy went back to work, as you all know,
In order to maintain the status quo.

Now with one child they must decide
If another baby they can abide.

Dating and courtship, love and marriage
Your perspective changes when pushing a baby carriage.

Moonlight

The full moon occurred in mid-October
It shines bright without cloud cover.

When the moon is full there are those that say
Lovers and others will go astray.

Though it's not proven as an actual fact
There have been many an unusual act.

It could be innocence, drugs or alcohol
It could be any one or combination of all.

These things happen, try as we might
We must be responsible in the moonlight.

Mel Negaard

Moonlight Romances

The lovers strolled under a full moon,
Hand in hand and ready to spoon.

He started humming then began to croon,
The love song about a bride and groom.

He got on his knee and said, he'd be the groom
If she'd be the bride, they would marry soon.

Your proposal she said is a bit too soon,
Ask me again when there is no full moon.

The both agreed it was too soon
And needed time for their love to bloom.

There were bright times and a little gloom
The compromises were small and their love did bloom.

Now love in full flower the bride and groom
They were married under the full moon.

Belonging

A man and woman they did meet
And had a romance which was very discrete

She was a beauty he was a handsome man
They sealed their vows with a wedding band

Time went by and a child did arrive
It appeared that the marriage would survive

The child they had was a baby boy
To parents and relatives he brought much joy

It seems that jealousy on the father's part
At least temporarily drew them apart

If the parental bond is sufficiently strong
The family will reunite that's where they belong.

Mel Negaard

Maiden's Lament

The Weekend is here and it's Saturday night.
A nice night out would be a delight.

She sits close to the telephone and makes a call,
But no one is home, she will miss the Ball.

She's all dressed up and ready to go.
There was one call but it was a no-no.

Now it's too late and a time to dread
So takes her book and goes to bed.

Next weekend, perhaps there is a man of means
That will fulfill her fantasy dreams.

Guts

For a good physique just breathe in and out
And as you do so hold in your gut.

Now as you breathe with stomach muscles taught
The air expands the chest, as the lungs ought.

With an expanded chest you stand more erect
And your physique becomes more correct.

So for a nice figure get out of the rut
Take a deep breath and pull in your gut.

Mel Negaard

Marriage

When couples marry and the passion's high
Their dreams soar high in the sky.

Their many dreams, of little consequence
Are because our dreams have no substance.

As the marriage ages and kids leave the nest
Parents get a break and get some rest.

Then the grandkids come back to roost
And Grandma and Pa will need a boost.

How do you boost those who retire?
Winning the lotto was their desire.

And so Granny, come and stay
We love you; don't go away.

The Feminists

The Amazon woman was a feminist plot
To maintain dominion over their tribal lot
Males were not breast fed, that was the rule,
And was not considered by them to be cruel.

Food was given to them in small portions
To keep them diminutive in physical proportions
This was their way of maintaining dominance
Over all the males in their province.

There is a movement, some protagonists say,
The feminists are coming and bring moral decay
Should we males just stand by
And give the gals a good old college try?

In their endeavors where will we be
Living in clover or facing poverty?
Perhaps the feminists can show us how
To correct the things we're doing wrong now.

Those Amazon gals, with much at stake,
With all their wisdom made a big mistake
They excluded males when they legislate
And leave them out and not on their slate.

Now after you have read this poem
Consider the message when you get home
The Amazonian women…they had their game
Is that what you want…more of the same?

Mel Negaard

Full Circle

There is a saying that is profound
And that message is: "what goes around comes around".

For years the gays were very discrete
And now they are on the street.

Years ago they used to cloak it,
Until they opened the door of the closet.

Now the teenagers with chew or smoke it
Are driven back into the closet.

Now this causes some people anxiety.
What ever happened to our society?

He'n And She'n

In this world is many a country.
Some act acceptably and some are contrary.

In some countries women are bare-breasted,
In other countries they'd be arrested.

Here, in our country, some gals and guys,
Want all of us to recognize

That it may be genetic that women love women,
Or, by the same token, that men love men.

If this continues to the extreme,
What does it tell us, what does it mean?

With no procreation; there is no rebirth,
That could end man's life here on Earth.

Mel Negaard

AIDS Vs Asylums

We have a problem in this modern age
It has to do with HIV and then AIDS

We dealt with other diseases like TB
And had asylums for them and leprosy

The AIDS situation will become chronic
Unless we stop thinking it's economic

If not curbed soon there will be one of three
That will include some of our family

So the question is are we ready
To create asylums to protect society

Sexuality

It is only natural when our mothers gave us birth
That we were destined then to live upon this earth.

It is Mother Nature, who determines the sexes,
But sexual preferences altered our reproductiveness.

The earth is over-populated; that we know for sure,
But we think homosexuality will not be the cure.

The tale of Sodom and Gomorra the Bible does relate;
How they did live and what was their awful fate.

Now we have HIV and AIDS. Is this Nature's way, in sexual relation,
To control the earth's population?

Mel Negaard

The U.S.A. Armed Forces

The Army, Navy, Air force, the Coast Guard and Marines
When we joined up we didn't know what all it means.

We passed basic training or Navy/Marine Boot
So we should be ready to go on a toot.

Now listen up you volunteers in service
If you do wrong, beware of the consequence.

Though military code you did not know
Things in the book at you they can throw.

You guys and gals must not fraternize
For to the military you cannot apologize.

The sexual urges of male and female
In the military it shall not prevail.

When you are on leave and not in uniform
To the military code you still must conform.

Before you volunteers try to proposition
Ask your sexual partner if there is a military condition.

If rank is equal, it is okay
If it is not, there will be hell to pay.

Military code to you volunteers in the ranks
If you break the barrier, for service there's no thanks.

For you it's court martial that is imminent
Even though you're a volunteer, the punishment is permanent.

Who Harassed Who

Harassment should be to men the same,
When it is women that are to blame.

When a woman approaches and blinks her eyes,
It seems to dazzle most of the guys.

Then he asks her, just on a hunch,
If she would like to go out for lunch.

And if her waist his arm is around,
For sexual harassment he can be found.

But if a woman makes suggestive poses,
Where are the charges? Who sent the roses?

Men are not as thin skinned,
As those women who have sinned.

It is my opinion men don't go to court,
For sex harassment of this sort.

VIII

Games & Cars

Billiards

As a farm boy, high school was in town;
But in the spring the school burned down.
So as a freshman classes were less hours a day,
That gave us lots of time to play.
There were two pool halls we thought were great,
And that is where we would congregate.

Eight ball was a nickel, other games a dime,
But this was in the Depression time.
There were no laws not to smoke or chew,
If that is what you wanted to do.
In later life, after a divorce or two,
I took up the game and could compete with you.

Now I am old but let me tell you,
Just how good I used to be.
That is in the past, there is no proof,
Y'all just yawn and think it's a spoof.
Some family members, per their adventure,
I did quite well as an amateur.

Dreamers

Your spouse's ticket won the lottery,
And should be shared equally.

The spouse can say it was my money,
So get lost, this belongs to me.

Now was it good luck winning the lottery,
If it breaks up a happy family?

Winning the lotto is really a dream,
But may bring problems that are unforeseen.

The tickets we buy and winning would seem,
That we had fulfilled our most wondrous dream.

Mel Negaard

Lotto in Chicago

It is a lottery called the Power Ball
You can participate, come one, come all.

You have a chance one in 80 million,
But the big prize is $190 million.

It was in Wisconsin the town of Pell Lake
That the ticket was bought and the media did congregate.

The media was there and going to and fro
Looking for the winner of the biggest lotto.

The ticket was bought in this little town
All the media had to do is run it down.

The media's search with all their gear,
Hoping they would find the winner here.

But there is one thing they did not know
That the lotto winner lives in Chicago.

The World Series
(Padres VS Yankees)

The Padres ball team, early in the season,
Could not win by any rhyme or reason.

But when it was to the N/L west playoffs
The odds makers at the Padres did scoff.

After the Padres won the N/L west,
They had to face the Braves to see who is the best.

The Padres prevailed—we shouted yippee!
Now we will face the venerable Yankee.

It will be a contest against the Yankee might
But we all know the Padres will fight.

The teams will compete to the last inning
And that will determine which one ends up winning.

Whichever team wins four out of seven in their area
Will bring on baseball hysteria.

Wearing the crown is for one team
But next season is another club's dream.

Mel Negaard

Spike's Slough

There had been the winter snow and spring rain.
I was driving country roads over muddy terrain.

Muskrats in the pond had tunneled in the road.
That's where they lived; that was their abode.

It was Saturday night and after the dance
We brothers did not score; we wanted another chance.

We needed more gas from Dad's gas barrel.
That is when everything went to hell.

I got off track where I shouldn't "oughter,"
Hit the muskrat tunnel and drove off in the water.

Since I was driving, and this is true,
It is now known by our sisters as "Spike's Slough".

The Orange Crate

In '46 I was home from WW Two
What in the world was I going to do?

I was back on the farm with the family.
A vehicle for transportation was a necessity.

In post war years cars were worn-out.
You either fixed the old ones or you'd wipe out.

When in Chicago I bought an orange van.
I fixed it up as best as I can.

It was rusted and in disrepair,
But with some work it was better than fair.

For several years it roamed our county
And did not pay any bounty.

Until the day I passed on the wrong side—the Cop was there
At the curb I was told to pay my fare.

Now I know at this late date
Why they called it my "Orange Crate".

Mel Negaard

The Look Alikes

Years ago, as a kid, all the cars I knew
By the make or model—whatever, old or new.

It is true less models were made back then,
But when will it stop?—please tell me when.

Now all the makes have similar shapes
From the wind tunnel tests, cars made from computer tapes.

My neighbor bought a brand new car
A Cadillac or Hyundai, not known from near or far.

So tell me where the identity has gone
When the car you drive—the make is unknown.

Wheels

It's true the Americans live on their wheels,
And even the poor can make auto deals.

Many of our products come on 18-wheelers
To deliver merchandise to their authorized dealers.

They travel cross-country thru wind, snow and rains
And some trailers even come on trains.

Using their cars and RV's for special occasions,
Many are also used on their vacations.

We also have wheels for other applications:
All farm machinery is moved to various locations.

"Invention of the wheel," stated a noted sage,
"Brought the world into the mechanized age."

Mel Negaard

Ode to the Gull

My car is bright and shiny although it is old,
But it starts when it is warm as well as when it's cold.
I drove it to the beach and parked it in the lot
Every gull that flew over left its own spot!

Two hours later my car was messed up
I got out water and a mop
The car is now clean though progress was slow
Until the next time to the beach I go.

IX

Celebrations, Troubles & Empathy

Congratulations
(It is a Boy/Girl)

The day you were born everyone was glad,
And this was special for your mother and dad.

The parents provide the tender care,
The nurturing and love that is needed there.

As grandparents, we want to see
The grandchild that is our progeny.

Congratulations.

Happy Anniversary

They were a lovely couple, they were a good match.
Each of them thought, they made a good catch.
The marriage was planned for later that year,
But with the hugs and kisses the waiting they could not bear.

So in February they tied the knot,
One flower in the bouquet was a Forget-me-not.
A marriage made in heaven, yea, a heavenly dream,
And ever since then it has been peaches and cream.

As you get older and romance fades,
Do not forget the good old days.

Mel Negaard

Home Sweet Home

Owning your own home is such a delight
But when catastrophe hits, it's such a fright
As for instance my plumbing started to leak
I was not home for at least a week

It ruined the carpet and part of the wall
It got in the bathroom as well as the hall
I called my insurance and for him to make haste
To give me an estimate for cleaning up the waste

Then came the selection of new carpet and flooring
Making all these decisions sent my blood pressure soaring
With the decisions made and the repairs done
I have time to lean back or go into town

This is my home, this is where I reside
With the next catastrophe I think I will go and hide
With owning a home comes responsibility
And having problems is a reality

Post Graduation

After graduation more is required
If the good life for you is desired.

At least Jr. College or a trade school
Will make a difference in the labor pool.

Now as a graduate, can you abide?
For in the real world there is no free ride.

For in this life it is not a whim
For each of us it is sink or swim.

Now is the time your future to consider
Will it be fruitful or will it wither.

Let it be fruitful throughout the years
And may it be happy not full of tears.

Making right choices good friends we keep
And a beautiful life we will reap.

In this verse and in this plan,
Adhere to it if you can.

Go for it!

Mel Negaard

Recovering

When you have a stroke it can be devastating
Some have difficulty doing the simplest thing.

Whatever part of the brain is afflicted
Determines the muscles affected.

Many times it effects more than one area
Families be patient and avoid hysteria.

The lack of speech and of mobility;
The brain can compensate for this disability.

It will take time, there is no doubt,
Before you talk and are getting about.

With a lot of fortitude and a strong will
You will recover and get well.

The Silent World

In the silent world there is no sound
There is nary a decibel that can be found,

If you are awaiting some words from home
It will not be by using a telephone

You must read and write in order to communicate
You must learn these skills or you will vegetate

Without sound there is no radio
By the same token there is no stereo

So be compassionate next time you are near
Any of those people who cannot hear.

Mel Negaard

Pleasantries

When I was younger and in good health
Even in adversity could care for myself.

Now getting older and infirmities set in
The spirit is there but the muscles cave in.

There are many things such as a small task
Where someone helps even though you don't ask.

The pleases and thank yous will go a long way
To provide everyone a more pleasant day.

I know this to be so true
And it will work as well for you.

The "Golden Years"

We are homebodies 'cept to Doc and store
Waiting for loved ones to knock on the door.

We don't entertain as we did before
The bones are brittle and muscles are sore.

The aging process and its maladies
Have invaded our vulnerable aging bodies.

But come and visit or give us a call
For we love you and news from y'all.

X

Calendar in Poetry

Our Calendar

It was Gregory who figured it out,
Of what the seasons were all about.

It was out of step he did think,
For the seasons it was out of sync.

He added two months and changed the days,
And the months were named in other ways.

Caesar Agustus said Greg lookie here,
Put my name on your calendar.

The seventh month was called September,
And the eighth month was called October.

November and December, the end of the year,
Gregory kept them in his new calendar.

1998 and Beyond

The year is 1997 is in the past
And the New Year is here at last.

Now is the time for a New Year resolution
Though in most cases it is not the solution.

We look forward to good times and health
And to ask for prosperity and wealth.

To each of us may this be true
Starting in January and all the year through.

When this new year ends and '99 does arrive
We give thanks that we are still alive.

Happy New Year!

Mel Negaard

'99 A New Year

Nineteen Ninety Eight is in the past
And the New Year is here at last.

The joys and sorrows of the past year
May bring laughter or may shed a tear.

With the New Year many make resolutions,
Who have problems and seek solutions.

That is a start—a good beginning
And if successful, bells will be ringing

But if your goal you did not attain
At least you tried and can try again.

We are all mortal and not always right
But we cling to life with all our might.

HAPPY NEW YEAR

Hello — Goodbye
(What is Time?)

Where is it from—where does it go?
Sometimes it's fast then again it's slow.

As the earth spins at its steady rate
Each time zone passes not early or late.

The days go by and also the years
And our lives progress with joy and tears.

As we look towards two thousand and one
May God bless the century newly begun.

Mel Negaard

Y2K (Bah Humbug) 12/99

I am a Country Boy and computer illiterate.
As for Y2K—I didn't consider it.

Now Maybe the computers will hiccough or glitch,
Or perhaps perform without even a hitch.

The experts conclude we are not to worry
If there are problems they will fix them in a hurry.

Transportation will be safe, and so is your money;
But if they are wrong it won't be funny.

All this computer talk—is it just a ploy?
Who needs them anyway. I'm just a Country Boy.

The Presidential Month

This is the month of the Presidents
And is celebrated by most residents.

George Washington chopped down the cherry tree
And he was truthful; honest as can be.

Abraham Lincoln worked in a store returning an overcharge,
Walked nine miles or more.

Our Presidents are to be revered
With our constitution none should be feared.

Laws of the land apply to all of us
From the most influential down to the lowliest

In this presidential month Congress may beseech
There is evidence the President to impeach.

With impeachment that is the score;
We wind up with vice-president Gore.

This Presidential month could set a precedent
Of how to impeach a sitting President.

The three branches of our Government
Our Representatives swear to uphold the covenant.

Though the Presidential problems continue to thrive;
As a nation we will survive.

This Presidential month, it may be written
That is the demise of President Clinton.

Mel Negaard

February Events

There is a day that is set aside,
To show your love to your friend or bride.

You can give a card or a hug or two,
Whatever you choose, it is up to you.

The love you show will linger and stay,
The whole year through 'till next Valentines Day.

Another day we celebrate that is a national event,
To honor all the men who have been president.

It is also winter and there is plenty of snow,
If not where you live, you've not far to go.

I almost forgot about Ground Hog's Day,
If there's a shadow, our winter will stay.

When February is over and also winter's sting,
We can look forward to a pleasant spring.

Love Vs Hate

Four letter words such as love and hate
Can be powerful or can be innate.

We can hate the way one dresses
Or the way they leave messes.

But real hate goes much deeper
Such as victims of incest and murder.

Love is different—its a two way street
It is hugging and kissing and is very sweet.

Love and hate can be an adjective
But be careful of your objective.

Love by example can help you make
A better person of one you used to hate.

It is on Valentine's Day and the flight of the Dove
That we give expressions of our heartfelt love.

HAPPY VALENTINE'S DAY

Mel Negaard

March

This is the month the winds do blow,
That helps the sun melt the winter snow.

The ides of March, Caesar said beware,
We must face it and take the dare.

Later in the month is the first day of spring,
And thoughts of gardening it should bring.

It is also the time where day equals night,
It is the equinox so that is all right.

With March over, and it's trivial,
We look forward to the month of April.

The Green and Gold

On St. Patrick's Day it means wearing green,
And you better too, when making a scene.

There are Irish stories we have been told,
When finding a leprechaun, you get a pot of gold.

Searching for him there is no ban,
He says find me if you can.

Mel Negaard

Spring — Etc.
March 2001

In California it is now Spring
And the planting is in full swing.

The early Flowers are in full bloom
And the vegetable plants need more room.

The early veggies will come and go
But we must wait for a ripe tomato.

To glean the harvest after the Spring seeding
There is the chore of arduous weeding.

But in the Winter and our sumptuous eating
Who does remember the arduous weeding?
ME!

April

It starts out with all fools day,
Playing a fun joke on friends is okay.

It is the time in the dirt to dig,
And envision your plants growing nice and big.

You watch them grow and you pull the weeds,
Apply fertilizer according to their needs.

We must also remember to give to the IRS,
For if we forget they'll be after us.

Now that it is over and we paid our tax,
For another year we can lean back and relax.

Mel Negaard

April
(Easter and Showers)

April first is all fool's day.
No fool like an old fool, is what they say

For the next year, let's play it cool
So we will not be called an April fool.

For the gardeners—you should be planning
The vegetables and flowers you will be planting.

April second is Good Friday.
And on April fourth is Easter Day

The Protestants will gather in mass
And the Catholics will have high mass.

At the church service commitments are made
And in New York it's the Easter Parade

New finery bought on credit or paid
Will be worn to be displayed.

We receive compliments at the parade
But isn't it a part of the charade?

The day after, we face real life
With daily chores, problems and strife.

So this is April with its April showers.
Let us look forward to the May flowers.

Spring Has Sprung

We know its spring when the orioles arrive.
It is time to plant tomatoes and also the chive.

The hummers and finches they come first,
Then come the orioles with an urgent thirst.

The garden plantings will flower soon,
A bountiful harvest would be a boon.

We must be aware that insects may infest
And for insecticides we must invest.

Now we can glean the fruits of our labor
To smell their freshness and to taste their flavor.

Summer is gone and harvest is past,
After a long winter it is spring at last!

Mel Negaard

Wild Flowers

For millions of years
Mother Nature does provide

A variety of blossoms
All over the countryside.

Some years they are scarce
Other times are plentiful

You may just get a bouquet
Or at times a bucketful.

The flower produces seeds
That are for regeneration

That guarantees survival
For generation after generation.

Though they have bloomed
For eons in the past

We are the ones
Who have viewed them last.

May Days

Now we have the month of May
When we have many a beautiful day.

There is the fauna and also the flowers
And the activities of the farmers.

Planting the corn and also the wheat
Hoping the harvest will be sweet.

The college students think May is great
For this is the month when they will graduate.

Then Memorial Day will come real soon
Now get ready for the month of June.

Mel Negaard

May

On the first of May you didn't ask it,
To your best friend you gave a May basket.

A basket you made with paper and glue,
Filled with candy or flowers showed that I like you.

There is a day this month we reserve,
For the many people that their country did serve.

To those that served and died we pray,
As we honor them on Memorial Day.

You Are Special

It takes a baby and its father,
For you to become a mother.

Household chores, one thing or another,
That's the way it is after becoming a mother.

The years go by and life is humdrum,
But that's the way it is after becoming a mom.

For one day each year you can be happy and gay,
That is when we celebrate your very special day.

Happy Mother's Day!

Mel Negaard

To: Ma, MaMa, Mom, and Mothers

The women who have children
Do not consider them as a burden.

When they hurt she hears their cries
And comes to wipe tears from their eyes.

On special occasions there is a present
Given to them from a loving parent.

A Mother's love—it is profound
Unlike any other that can be found.

A Mother is proud of her offspring
For drawings, flowers or most anything.

Thank you, Mother for helping me to grow
And that is why I love you so.

Now, one thing more, just let me say
To all you Mothers on your special day:

HAPPY MOTHER'S DAY

June

When May is over with Mother's Day
We also observed Memorial Day.

And now with the coming of June
There will be weddings and also the Honeymoon.

Also, this month we honor Dad
With ties and socks he needs real bad!

The sun on the mountains melts the winter snow
And floods the lands that are far below.

The rays of the sun on the seeds we sow
And the gentle rains make the plants grow.

That's all for June; end of story
The words for July will be more poetry.

Mel Negaard

June — Seeds to Sow

The days are warm and the seeds we did sow,
We weed and water and watch them grow.

Songbirds are back and they are nesting,
And soon their eggs will be hatching.

On Flag Day we are not at a loss,
To give tribute to Betsy Ross.

It is on the 21st that summer is here,
And also the longest day of the year.

It is also a time that church bells ring,
And the groom gives the bride a wedding ring.

It is vacation, the kids out of school,
They can run and play or swim in the pool.

My kids Call Me Dad

As a husband, so it seems
That your wife was the girl of your dreams.

With your first child you were so proud
That you could have shouted out loud.

Now being a father you have the responsibility
Of loving and caring for your family.

There will be times when life is the berries
But no one is promised a bowl of red cherries.

There were good times and you were riding high
Now in fond reflection you can lean back and sigh.

To all the fathers on this special day
We all wish you a Most Happy Father's Day.

Mel Negaard

Being A Father

It is more than planting the sperm,
You must consider the long term.

The mother and child need loving care,
And it is for you to pay their fare.

Through the terrible two's and the cries in the night,
You must be there to calm their fright.

In the formative years, you must be their guide,
Not disappear or go and hide.

Through the teens until on their own,
They will be living at your home.

Having said that, need I go farther?
By now you should know about being a father.

Happy Papa's Day!

July — Celebration

Crossing the Delaware colonial troops came down,
Defeating the British and the royal crown.

Taxation without representation we do not tolerate,
So on the 4th of July we do celebrate.

The farmers watch the corn grow tall,
And look forward to the harvest in the fall.

The thunderstorms bring showers of rain,
And the farmers start harvesting their grain.

Time marches on, this is not in jest,
Next thing we know it will be August.

Mel Negaard

July — Jubilation

The Month of July is one of Jubilation.
The 4th is Independence Day with Parades and Celebration.

The British Crown overtaxed the Tea.
And the Colonists (Indians) tossed it in the Sea.

We have been told it started the Revolution
And the Colonists sought a solution.

At Valley Forge and Crossing the Delaware,
General Washington caught the British unaware.

The Colonists won! It was a British insult.
And 13 States was the result.

Now we are Fifty States strong;
But, have our leaders led us wrong?

There was Korea after World War II,
Vietnam, France and Yugoslavia too.

Why doesn't NATO pay it's fair share,
When we furnish 80% of the hardware?

The European Countries will benefit more
If NATO can stop the expanded war.

I've rambled on for this month of July,
And that is enough for both you and I.

August

The Gregorian calendar is quite a rout
In that he changed the months about.

October used to be the eighth month of the year
Until Augustus Caesar said, "Now looky here,

If you change the calendar, put my name in there."

So Gregory moved September back
Which also threw October out of whack.

The old calendar was in disarray
And Earth's orbit it did not display.

Names of the months they did not track
But Gregory's calendar keeps the seasons intact.

Mel Negaard

September '98

Pre-Gregorian, the months were ten.
Now, September is month nine, not seven.

It was last year that Septuplets did arrive
And we hope they will all survive.

The first Monday is Labor Day
It is a long weekend ending summer's play.

Now it is back to school to gain the knowledge
That is required to enter college.

It's the Equinox and summer is ending.
Now is the season for the fall beginning.

Now we recognize that summer is over.
Look at the fall colors of the month of October.

It's September

Autumn is here, the grain is in the bin;
Next we will bring the corn crop in.

The cattle are in and the hay's in the mow;
We are all set for the winter snow.

Fruit and veggies, canning's complete,
Ready for all this winter to eat.

Jack Frost turns leaves red, gold and brown
To let us all know he has come around.

He wants us to know that winter near
And those snowstorms will soon be here;

Along with north winds that winter will bring
While we all await the blossoms of spring.

Mel Negaard

The Fall Season

Summer is past and fall is here;
Some say it is the best time of the year.

There is grain in the bin and hay in the barn
Activity is slower out on the farm.

The days are shorter and the nights longer
It gives us more time our futures to ponder.

This time of year leaves turn red and gold
Before they drop into the winter's cold.

So enjoy the fall and it's colorful hues
Before Mr. Winter brings bad news.

October — Indian Summer

This is the month of Indian Summer.
This is the time man is a hunter.

If game is scarce, he hunts much harder
To put the food in his larder.

And the winter wood, it should be stowed
To guard against the winter cold.

There are tricks and treats we must remember
Before we enter the month of November.

Mel Negaard

October — Early Fall 2000

A summer ends so does September
And the Fall begins as does October.

The sportsmen now get out their gun
For hunting season has just begun.

The tree leaves are changing color.
With a white frost just around the corner.

For the anglers, Fishing is for the robust,
But one last trip is almost a must.

Canning season over and proud of themselves,
The housewives can gaze at the food on the shelves.

The month of October has its Indian Summer,
But the snow will fall before the end of November.

October — Jack Frost

It is fall and Jack Frost is near
It can get cold this time of year.

The leaves on the trees are no longer green
They are multi-colored with a rich sheen.

The hunters go out with their bow or rifle
But to bag the game is no trifle.

The mountain peaks are dusted with snow
And the pine trees will no longer grow.

Harvest the corn and the pumpkins too
The children will want to carve one or two.

With Halloween over at the end of October,
We all move on to the month of November.

Mel Negaard

Thanks — Then and Now

When the Pilgrims landed at Plymouth Rock
In their larders was very little stock.

The Indians helped the Pilgrims to survive
The first year and kept them alive.

In the spring Pilgrims planted the fields
And in the autumn the crops did yield.

The Pilgrim's appreciation for their Indian friends
Wanted to share the harvest and to make amends.

The Indians were invited to the feast that day.
Then as now is called Thanksgiving Day.

A Pilgrim's Friend

It is November and not in May
That we celebrate Thanksgiving Day.

The Pilgrims decided after a bountiful year
That they give thanks and with the Indians share.

The Indians helped them when the years were bare
So they were invited their dinner to share.

Wild deer and turkey was on their dishes
When the feast was over there were many good wishes.

As it was then, it's much the same today
So have a very happy Thanksgiving day.

Mel Negaard

Six Months of Winter

On the northern plains it happens in the fall
And it occurs before the snowfall.

It comes to the area like a thief in the night
He is called Jack Frost and leaves everything white.

A month or so later the north winds blow
And the temperatures drop leaving a blanket of snow

The snow will continue until late spring
And it will cover almost everything.

The drifts will be high and the snowplows busy
If you are not strong it will make you dizzy.

The snow shovels have no rust
For shoveling a path is an essential must.

Whether to outhouse or to the street
There is no one who considers it a treat.

The winter drags on and at 40 below
The car won't start so we can't go.

In late spring it starts to thaw
And all the people give a big hurrah!

After spring and summer the fall will begin
And we can start all over again.

December — Businesses Smile

Now the bells ring Jingle Bell Rock
And businesses smile as they sell their stock

To buy the gifts for relatives or a pard'
You just present your credit card

The gifts are opened on Christmas day
You will be saluted but have a year to pay

The credit card companies they are smiling too
Awaiting cost and interest that are due

To your surprise you've been suckered into
A buyer's trap you cannot undo

That's not true, as you can see
You can always file for bankruptcy

Mel Negaard

Gifts and Spirit

Santa has been busy and with all his elves
Has made many toys and filled all the shelves

In the North Country he uses his sleigh
At Christmas Island it's a canoe in the Bay

The Christmas spirit, no matter the weather
It is great when we all get together

The gifts Santa brings are a reflection
Of a loved ones deep affection

It doesn't have to be gifts we are sharing
But let it also be loving and caring

The Prince of Peace

A baby boy God did create
And on His birthday all Christians celebrate

He was born to be God's only son
And He is the light to all Christendom.

This has been so for two thousand years
And has survived through wars and fears.

The Christians survived, only God knows how,
Perhaps divine intervention or the sacred vow.

We give homage to Christians who died
And to the faithful that have survived.

On Christmas day the Devil's on a leash
As we honor the birth of the Prince of Peace

Mel Negaard

Love and Caring
(The Spirit of Christmas)

This time of year is for Love and sharing,
Not for commercialization or gifts you are bearing

The gifts presented are merely a token
And should be savored as Love ties unbroken

The smallest gift may mean much more,
With the Love it brings, than any other will score

So this Holiday Season, be one of sharing
Not for commercialization, but for Love and Caring

Happy Holidays

0-595-31174-1